THE POETRY OF RUTHENIUM

The Poetry of Ruthenium

Walter the Educator

SKB

Silent King Books a WhichHead Imprint

Copyright © 2023 by Walter the Educator

All rights reserved. No part of this book may be reproduced in any manner whatsoever without written permission except in the case of brief quotations embodied in critical articles and reviews.

First Printing, 2023

Disclaimer
This book is a literary work; poems are not about specific persons, locations, situations, and/or circumstances unless mentioned in a historical context. This book is for entertainment and informational purposes only. The author and publisher offer this information without warranties expressed or implied. No matter the grounds, neither the author nor the publisher will be accountable for any losses, injuries, or other damages caused by the reader's use of this book. The use of this book acknowledges an understanding and acceptance of this disclaimer.

"Earning a degree in chemistry changed my life!"
– Walter the Educator

dedicated to all the chemistry lovers, like myself, across the world

CONTENTS

Dedication v

Why I Created This Book? 1

One - Ruthenium Shines 2

Two - Beyond Compare 4

Three - Remarkable Glory 6

Four - Hidden Gem 8

Five - Boundless Measure 10

Six - Science To Style 12

Seven - Element Divine 14

Eight - Awe And Embrace 16

Nine - Eternal Light 18

Ten - Ruthenium, The Enigmatic 20

Eleven - Wonders Of This Earth 22

Twelve - Solace And Care 24

Thirteen - Rise Above	. . . .	26
Fourteen - Warrior Against Cancer	. . . . .	28
Fifteen - Magic Beholds	. . . .	30
Sixteen - Wonders Of This World	. . . . . .	32
Seventeen - Forever Adore	. . . .	34
Eighteen - Ruthenium, The Muse	. . . .	36
Nineteen - Gift Of Grace	. . . .	38
Twenty - Leave Your Brand	. . . .	40
Twenty-One - Essence Divine	. . . .	42
Twenty-Two - Metal Of Myriad Charms	. . .	44
Twenty-Three - Symbol Of Strength	. . . . . .	46
Twenty-Four - Passion Takes Wings	. . . . .	48
Twenty-Five - Secrets Untangled	. . . .	50
Twenty-Six - Power And Thy Grace	. . . . .	52
Twenty-Seven - Your Versatility	. . . .	54
Twenty-Eight - You Captivate	. . . .	56
Twenty-Nine - Pain And Sorrow	. . . .	58
Thirty - Enthralling Thrall	. . . .	60
Thirty-One - A Treasure	. . . .	62
Thirty-Two - Old And New	. . . .	64

Thirty-Three - Reaching The Skies 66

Thirty-Four - Leaving A Trace 68

Thirty-Five - Masterpiece 70

About The Author 72

WHY I CREATED THIS BOOK?

Creating a poetry book about the chemical element Ruthenium was an intriguing and unique endeavor. Ruthenium, with its atomic number 44, symbol Ru, and diverse range of properties, offers a rich source of inspiration. Through poetry, I can explore the various aspects of Ruthenium, such as its historical significance, physical and chemical properties, and its role in different fields like catalysis and electronics. This book could delve into themes of transformation, rarity, beauty, and the relationship between science and art. It is an innovative way to merge science and creativity, appealing to both science enthusiasts and poetry lovers.

ONE

RUTHENIUM SHINES

In the depths of Earth, a hidden treasure lies,
A metal rare, that catches every eye,
Ruthenium, its name, a mystery untold,
A story of elements, forever to unfold.

In nature's lab, where stars collide,
Ruthenium emerges, a beauty to reside,
A gleaming metal, with lustrous grace,
Enchanting atoms, in a cosmic embrace.

A symbol of strength, in its atomic shell,
Ruthenium's secrets, it will never tell,
A noble metal, with a heart so pure,
Radiating brilliance, forever to endure.

From jewelry to science, it finds its way,
In catalysts and alloys, it holds sway,

A catalyst of change, in chemical reactions,
Unraveling the mysteries, with scientific attractions.
    In the depths of labs, where scientists explore,
Ruthenium's power, they truly adore,
From solar cells to cancer drugs,
Its potential, like a million hugs.
    A metal of wonder, a symbol of might,
Ruthenium shines, like a star in the night,
Unveiling the secrets of the universe,
A gift to mankind, a blessing, not a curse.
    So let us marvel at Ruthenium's grace,
A precious element, in this cosmic space,
For in its atoms, a story unfolds,
Of a metal rare, that forever holds.

TWO

BEYOND COMPARE

In the depths of the periodic table's embrace,
Lies a treasure hidden, with grace and with grace.
Ruthenium, oh element of might and of power,
A symbol of strength in every hour.

A catalyst for change, you silently reside,
Unveiling mysteries that the universe hides.
Your atoms dance, in a symphony of light,
Guiding us forward, through darkness and night.

In jewelry, you shimmer, a touch of allure,
Elegant adornments, so precious and pure.
Your lustrous presence, a sight to behold,
A story untold, within your atoms unfold.

In the realm of science, you take center stage,
A metal of wonders, with a wisdom of age.

In labs and experiments, your secrets unfurled,
Unveiling pathways to heal a wounded world.
    In medicine, you heal, with a gentle touch,
A guardian of health, we value so much.
Your essence, a healer, a promise of hope,
A remedy for ailments, helping us cope.
    Oh Ruthenium, your worth we extol,
A gem of the elements, with a captivating soul.
Unique and enchanting, your beauty so rare,
A symphony of atoms, beyond compare.

THREE

REMARKABLE GLORY

Ruthenium, a hidden treasure,
In the depths of the periodic chart.
A symbol of strength, a catalyst for change,
In the world of science and art.
Unassuming in its appearance,
A lustrous, silvery-gray hue.
Yet within its atomic heart,
A power, rare and true.
In the laboratory, it dances,
With other elements in a chemical waltz.
Creating compounds, unlocking secrets,
In science's ever-evolving vaults.
But beyond the walls of the lab,
Ruthenium finds its way,
Into the realm of precious jewelry,
Where its beauty holds sway.

Adorning rings and bracelets,
With a touch of elegance and grace,
Ruthenium captures the eye,
Leaving a lasting trace.

In medicine, it plays a role,
As a powerful ally,
Fighting cancer's relentless grip,
With determination and supply.

Oh Ruthenium, you captivate,
With your multifaceted charm.
A hidden gem, a force to be reckoned,
In the world's eternal arm.

So let us celebrate this element,
In all its remarkable glory.
For Ruthenium, you truly are,
A testament to nature's story.

FOUR

HIDDEN GEM

In shadows deep, where secrets sleep,
Lies Ruthenium, a metal rare,
A mystery clad in darkness' keep,
A silent force beyond compare.
 Within its core, a power untold,
A catalyst for change and might,
Where transformation takes its hold,
And dreams take flight under starlit night.
 In laboratories, scientists delve,
Unraveling its enigmatic ways,
With each discovery, they are compelled,
To marvel at its enigmatic maze.
 But Ruthenium's allure extends afar,
From lab to lands where beauty gleams,

In jewelry's embrace, a shining star,
It adorns with elegance and dreams.
    In medicine's realm, it lends its grace,
A healer's touch, a remedy's might,
With every dose, a life's new pace,
A glimmer of hope in darkest night.
    Oh Ruthenium, thy power profound,
In science and art, thy presence felt,
A hidden gem, in mysteries bound,
In jewelry and medicine, hearts are dealt.
    So let us cherish this metal rare,
With awe and wonder, let it shine,
For Ruthenium, beyond compare,
In secrets and potential, it's divine.

FIVE

BOUNDLESS MEASURE

In the realm of elements, there lies a gem,
A radiant metal, Ruthenium by name.
In the depths of science, its secrets stem,
A shimmering beauty, its claim to fame.

With a lustrous sheen, it graces the night,
A noble presence, a celestial sight.
In jewelry's embrace, it finds its place,
Adorning wrists, necks, and fingers with grace.

Its strength unmatched, a force to behold,
In alloys and compounds, its power unfolds.
A catalyst of change, a catalyst of dreams,
In labs and reactors, its magic streams.

But Ruthenium's allure extends beyond,
To the realm of medicine, where it responds.

From implants to drugs, it plays its part,
Healing and curing, a life-changing art.
    Yet, Ruthenium's charm lies not in its might,
But in its enigma, its mystery's light.
An element of wonder, transformative and true,
In art, science, jewelry, and medicine too.
    So let us celebrate this element divine,
Ruthenium, a jewel that forever shines.
In the tapestry of elements, a rare treasure,
A testament to nature's boundless measure.

SIX

SCIENCE TO STYLE

In the depths of the earth, a treasure lies,
A metal rare, with secrets in disguise.
Ruthenium, the enigma of the night,
Shining with a captivating light.

In laboratories, its power is unveiled,
A catalyst, where mysteries are hailed.
In chemical reactions, it takes its role,
Guiding transformations, making them whole.

In medicine's realm, a healer it becomes,
Fighting diseases with its potent drums.
Radiation therapy, a gift it brings,
Curing souls with its atomic wings.

A gem of science, its essence refined,
A symbol of knowledge, forever entwined.
But beyond the lab, its allure extends,
To the realm of beauty, where it transcends.

In jewelry's embrace, it finds its throne,
An adornment rare, with elegance known.
A dark luster, mysterious and deep,
A ring of Ruthenium, a secret to keep.
　　Oh, Ruthenium, your beauty so pure,
A shimmering jewel, forever endure.
From science to style, you gracefully blend,
A metal of wonders, till eternity's end.

SEVEN

ELEMENT DIVINE

In the depths of the earth's embrace,
A treasure lies, adorned with grace.
Ruthenium, a jewel sublime,
A symphony woven through space and time.
  With strength of steel, it claims its might,
A catalyst for change, shining bright.
In the crucible of science's fire,
It sparks the flames of hope and desire.
  From labs to factories, it lends its hand,
A silent hero, in every land.
Transforming elements, with magic untold,
Creating wonders, pure and bold.
  In medicine's realm, it finds its place,
A healer's touch, with gentle grace.

A whisper of life, a potent cure,
Ruthenium's power, forever pure.
    Oh, Ruthenium, your mysteries unfold,
A tale of wonder, never to grow old.
In jewelry's realm, you find your throne,
A symbol of elegance, to call our own.
    Silver and gold, entwined with your hue,
A dance of beauty, forever anew.
In precious adornments, you find your name,
A testament to your eternal flame.
    Ruthenium, oh element divine,
Your essence, like stars, forever shine.
In science, medicine, and jewelry's gleam,
You are the secret, the alchemist's dream.

EIGHT

AWE AND EMBRACE

In a realm of hidden wonders, where secrets lie untold,
There exists a precious element, a marvel to behold.
Ruthenium, enigmatic and rare, with a lustrous sheen,
A jewel among the elements, a treasure yet unseen.

From the depths of Earth's embrace, it emerges with grace,
A catalyst of transformation, a beacon in space.
Its atomic dance, a symphony of endless creation,
Unleashing its power, a catalyst of salvation.

In the realms of medicine, Ruthenium finds its place,
A healer of ailments, a balm for the human race.
With its touch, it binds the broken, mending hearts anew,
A remedy for suffering, a cure that rings true.

A companion to the stars, Ruthenium adorns the night,
Its brilliance in the cosmos, a celestial delight.
Embraced by the moon's glow, it sparkles and it gleams,
A cosmic jewelry, a beauty beyond our dreams.

Oh, Ruthenium, you captivate, with your mystique and allure,
A symbol of resilience, a treasure pure and sure.
In science, art, and wonder, your essence shines bright,
A testament to the marvels that lie within the night.

So let us raise our voices, in praise for Ruthenium's might,
A gift from the universe, a beacon of light.
In its presence, we find hope, in its essence, we find grace,
Ruthenium, the element, that leaves us in awe and embrace.

NINE

ETERNAL LIGHT

In the depths of Earth's embrace,
Lies a gem of radiant grace.
Ruthenium, a hidden treasure,
A metal of beauty without measure.

In jewelry, it finds its home,
A lustrous shine, it proudly owns.
Adorning necks and wrists so fine,
A testament to its design.

But beyond its ornate display,
Ruthenium dances in another way.
In medicine, it finds its role,
A healer, to soothe the soul.

Through catalysts, it transforms,
Molecules bend to its gentle norms.
A catalyst of life, it lends a hand,
Helping reactions in the chemical land.

From the lab to the surgeon's knife,
Ruthenium brings forth new life.
In cancer treatments, it holds a key,
A potent ally in therapy.

Oh, Ruthenium, enigmatic and true,
Your secrets unfold, a mystical hue.
A metal of wonder, a gift untold,
In your presence, mysteries unfold.

So let us marvel at your might,
And cherish your presence in our sight.
Ruthenium, a marvel, shining so bright,
A gift from nature's eternal light.

TEN

RUTHENIUM, THE ENIGMATIC

In the realm of elements, Ruthenium resides,
A metal rare, where beauty and mystery coincide.
Its lustrous shine, like moonlight on a winter's eve,
Entrancing hearts, its allure none can deceive.

In jewelry's embrace, Ruthenium finds its home,
Crafted into bands and necklaces, it loves to roam.
A majestic adornment, both sleek and refined,
Its presence on the skin, a treasure to find.

But Ruthenium's magic extends beyond mere flair,
Its healing touch, a gift that's incredibly rare.
In medicine's embrace, it lends a helping hand,
A catalyst for change, where miracles expand.

Yet Ruthenium's enigma, oh, it runs so deep,
Its secrets concealed, its essence hard to keep.

A noble metal, it stands with silent grace,
A symbol of strength, in its quiet embrace.
　From science's laboratory to nature's grand design,
Ruthenium weaves its tale, so wonderfully divine.
In every atom, in every molecule, it resides,
A cosmic beauty, where science and art collide.
　So let us celebrate this element so grand,
Ruthenium, the enigmatic, the elegant, the sand.
In jewelry's gleam, in medicine's healing touch,
This element of wonders, we cherish so much.

ELEVEN

WONDERS OF THIS EARTH

In the depths of the periodic table's embrace,
A noble element finds its rightful place.
Ruthenium, a catalyst of change,
In the alchemical realm, its powers arrange.

A healer, a mender, a whispering hand,
In medicine's realm, it takes a stand.
With radiance and grace, it mends the weak,
A soothing elixir, the body it seeks.

Through the veins, it courses, with grace it flows,
A catalyst of healing, where hope grows.
In the crucible of life, it holds the key,
Unlocking the secrets of vitality.

Yet Ruthenium's allure does not end there,
In jewelry's embrace, it shines so rare.

A darkened beauty, an enigmatic gleam,
Captivating hearts with an elegant theme.
   A precious metal, mysterious and bold,
Its essence captured in bands of gold.
Adorning fingers with a subtle grace,
A symbol of love that time cannot erase.
   Oh, Ruthenium, your powers so vast,
In science, in art, forever they'll last.
A catalyst for change, a healer's touch,
In jewelry's allure, you shine so much.
   So let us celebrate this element divine,
From the depths of the periodic line.
Ruthenium, a gem of such rare worth,
A testament to the wonders of this Earth.

TWELVE

SOLACE AND CARE

In the realm of elements, a jewel does persist,
Ruthenium, precious and enigmatic, I insist.
A metal of darkness, in the shadows it resides,
With powers untold, where secrets it hides.

A catalyst of change, it sparks the flame,
Guiding transformations in its noble name.
In the depths of chemistry, its wonders unfold,
A helper of reactions, both daring and bold.

But beyond the lab, a healer it becomes,
In radiation's embrace, it hums and thrums.
A guardian of health, a savior in disguise,
Fighting the battle, as hope it implies.

With its radiance, it adorns the night,
In jewelry it gleams, a mesmerizing sight.

A touch of elegance, a hint of grace,
Ruthenium's allure, none can replace.
    From science to art, its presence is felt,
A muse to creators, in every masterpiece dwelt.
Oh, Ruthenium, a marvel you are,
A symphony of elements, shining like a star.
    In your essence, a world of wonders unfold,
From catalyst to healer, a story untold.
Ruthenium, precious and rare,
In your embrace, we find solace and care.

THIRTEEN

RISE ABOVE

In the realm of elements, a catalyst supreme,
Ruthenium emerges, a poet's cherished theme.
With atomic grace, it weaves its intricate dance,
Igniting chemical reactions with a subtle, mesmerizing trance.

    A noble companion, it sparks a wondrous flame,
In laboratories, it finds its rightful claim.
Cancer's foe, it fights with might,
Unleashing hope in the darkest night.

    Its enigmatic nature, a secret it guards,
Science and art, in its essence, it regards.
From the periodic table, it casts a spell,
A magic elixir, no one can quell.

    In the alchemy of love, it shines so bright,
A symbol of devotion, a radiant light.

Adorning fingers, a ring of grace,
A testament to love, in every embrace.
 Like a guardian, it protects our health,
A silent warrior, bringing inner wealth.
In the night sky, its radiance gleams,
A star of elements, beyond our dreams.
 Oh, Ruthenium, so rare and true,
In your presence, we find something new.
A catalyst, a mystery, a symbol of love,
With every discovery, you rise above.

FOURTEEN

WARRIOR AGAINST CANCER

In the cosmic expanse, a starlet gleams,
A shimmering jewel, Ruthenium it seems.
With atomic grace, it dances in space,
A symbol of brilliance, an ethereal embrace.

Resilient it stands, amidst the celestial crowd,
A testament to strength, it whispers aloud.
Through fire and fury, it holds its ground,
A warrior of elements, never to be bound.

In the crucible of life, a catalyst it plays,
Igniting reactions, in mysterious ways.
A spark of potential, in every reaction,
Unleashing power, with a quiet satisfaction.

In the realm of healing, it finds its worth,
A warrior against cancer, a savior on Earth.

A beacon of hope, amidst darkness and pain,
Ruthenium, the warrior, a cure to regain.

An enigma it is, in science and art,
A puzzle unsolved, yet a masterpiece in part.
From laboratories to canvases, it leaves its mark,
A mystery to unravel, an enigmatic spark.

Oh, Ruthenium, you captivate our eyes,
With elegance and allure, you mesmerize.
A jewel in jewelry, a treasure so rare,
Healing properties, a gift beyond compare.

So let us celebrate, this element divine,
Ruthenium's brilliance, forever shall shine.
In the cosmic symphony, it takes its place,
A magical element, a beacon of grace.

FIFTEEN

MAGIC BEHOLDS

In the realm of elements, a treasure untold,
Lies Ruthenium, a metal, enigmatic and bold.
A catalyst of change, it dances with grace,
Unleashing reactions, in every chemical space.

In labs and in vials, its power it wields,
Igniting transformations, where innovation conceals.
From fuel cells to synthesizing drugs,
Ruthenium's touch, a catalyst that hugs.

But beyond the confines of scientific lore,
Ruthenium's secrets, go beyond the lab door.
In cancer's dark shadow, it lends a helping hand,
A warrior against the disease, that plagues the land.

Its atoms, like knights, fight with might,
Targeting tumors, in a valiant fight.
With precision and purpose, it takes its stand,
A beacon of hope, in the oncologist's hand.

Oh Ruthenium, you are more than you seem,
A symbol of strength, in science, and dream.
Your presence is felt, in art and in song,
An enigma, a mystery, that lingers for long.

From the canvas to the stage, your essence shines,
Infusing creativity, in intricate designs.
Oh Ruthenium, you captivate the soul,
A muse for the artists, who seek to unfold.

In the tapestry of elements, you're a gem,
A catalyst of change, a potent chemical emblem.
Ruthenium, oh Ruthenium, your story unfolds,
In science, art, and love, your magic beholds.

SIXTEEN

WONDERS OF THIS WORLD

In the depths of the periodic table's grand design,
A hidden gem of rarity doth shine,
Ruthenium, a name whispered in awe,
A mystery wrapped in an atomic glow.
    Born from the fiery heart of a dying star,
Its allure stretches galaxies afar,
A noble metal, steadfast and true,
With secrets that mankind yearns to pursue.
    In the lab, it dances with chemistry's might,
A catalyst, igniting reactions into the night,
Its atomic number hides a cosmic tale,
Of resilience and strength that will never fail.
    In the realm of science, it finds its place,
A puzzle piece in the vast cosmic space,

Unraveling mysteries, unlocking doors,
Expanding our knowledge, forevermore.
　But Ruthenium, oh, it does not confine,
Its beauty transcends the scientific line,
For in the world of art, it takes its flight,
Adorning canvases with shimmering light.
　In jewelry's embrace, it finds its allure,
A metal of elegance, so pure,
Embracing the skin with a gentle touch,
Captivating hearts, it enchants so much.
　Ruthenium, a symbol of the unseen,
A paradox, both strong and serene,
In science and art, its magic unfurls,
A testament to the wonders of this world.

SEVENTEEN

FOREVER ADORE

In the realm of elements, a jewel so rare,
Ruthenium, a beauty beyond compare.
A silent warrior in the depths of space,
With secrets unseen, it leaves no trace.

In laboratories, scientists delve,
Unveiling the wonders this metal can tell.
A catalyst of change, it sparks the flame,
Aiding reactions, igniting the game.

Yet Ruthenium's allure extends beyond,
To realms where art and beauty respond.
A brush dipped in ink, a canvas in hand,
Its essence captured, a masterpiece grand.

In the realm of love, Ruthenium shines,
A beacon of strength, a symbol refined.
It binds hearts together, unbreakable bond,
Through trials and tribulations, it carries on.

And in the realm of fashion, it takes its place,
Adorning jewelry with elegance and grace.
A pendant or ring, a subtle delight,
Reflecting the wearer's inner light.

Oh Ruthenium, mysterious and profound,
Your presence echoes without a sound.
In science, art, love, and fashion's domain,
You captivate and inspire, never in vain.

So let us raise a toast to this element rare,
Ruthenium, a treasure beyond compare.
May its brilliance guide us, forevermore,
In the realms it touches, forever adore.

EIGHTEEN

RUTHENIUM, THE MUSE

In realms of science, Ruthenium shines,
A beacon of discovery, its essence divine.
A metal of wonders, a catalyst supreme,
Unveiling secrets, in laboratories it gleams.

In art, Ruthenium finds its place,
A canvas of beauty, its grace embraced.
Its hues enchanting, like a mystic dance,
Painting masterpieces, a creator's trance.

In love's realm, Ruthenium weaves its spell,
An alchemist's touch, where hearts dwell.
Binding souls in an eternal embrace,
A symbol of passion, a love's true grace.

Now, let's explore Ruthenium anew,
Its healing powers, enigmatic and true.

A balm for wounds, a salve for pain,
Restoring spirits, like a gentle rain.

It whispers secrets, hidden deep within,
Uncovers mysteries, like a sacred hymn.
Unveiling paths, where healing flows,
Ruthenium's touch, a soothing repose.

Jewels adorned, with Ruthenium's embrace,
Shimmering with elegance, a celestial grace.
A precious treasure, cherished and rare,
Reflecting light, a radiance to share.

Catalyst of change, igniting the flame,
Transforming the ordinary, to a higher plane.
Inspiring minds, with its captivating spark,
Ruthenium, the muse, to creativity embark.

Raise a toast to Ruthenium, bold and true,
A symbol of strength, a treasure we pursue.
In science, art, love, and healing's embrace,
Ruthenium's presence, a marvel to trace.

NINETEEN

GIFT OF GRACE

In the realm of elements, a gem does shine,
Ruthenium, an enigma, so divine.
A dancer on the periodic stage,
With elegance and allure, it does engage.

A beacon of hope in the alchemist's quest,
Casting its light, a catalyst for the best.
A symbol of strength, forged in the fire,
Ruthenium's spirit, it will never tire.

In jewelry's embrace, it finds its home,
Adorning hearts, forever to roam.
A precious adornment, a shimmering prize,
Ruthenium's beauty, a love that never dies.

In fashion's realm, it paints a scene,
A hue of grace, both bold and serene.

Its touch on fabrics, a touch of charm,
Ruthenium's presence, a fashion alarm.
    In the cosmic symphony of elements,
Ruthenium's melody, the heart relents.
In the depths of stars, its atoms collide,
Creating new worlds, where dreams reside.
    Oh, Ruthenium, a mystery untold,
A song of creation, forever unfolds.
Inspiring minds, igniting the flame,
In your embrace, we'll forever acclaim.
    So let us celebrate this element rare,
For Ruthenium's magic, we all must share.
In science, art, love, and healing's embrace,
Ruthenium's essence, a gift of grace.

TWENTY

LEAVE YOUR BRAND

In the depths of the Earth, a hidden gem,
A treasure beyond compare, a radiant emblem.
Ruthenium, enigmatic and rare,
Unveiling its secrets with an enigmatic flair.

In the realm of science, its brilliance unfolds,
A catalyst for change, its story untold.
A beacon of hope, it guides us through,
Unveiling the mysteries, old and new.

Artistry it inspires, with hues so deep,
A muse to the painters, a secret to keep.
Its mesmerizing presence, a stroke of grace,
Unfolding magic, in every trace.

Fashion embraces its elegance and flair,
Adorning the world, with jewelry so rare.

Ruthenium's allure, forever shining bright,
A symbol of strength, a captivating sight.
  In healing's embrace, it finds its home,
A soothing balm, where troubles roam.
Its energy, gentle and serene,
Restoring balance, making hearts clean.
  Oh, Ruthenium, with power untold,
A star in the universe, a story to behold.
Forever captivating, forever grand,
In every realm, you leave your brand.

TWENTY-ONE

ESSENCE DIVINE

In the realm of art, its lustrous gleam,
Ruthenium reigns, a creator's dream.
A metal rare, a fiery spark,
Igniting passions in the deepest dark.

In jewelry's embrace, it finds its place,
Adornments crafted with delicate grace.
A precious allure, a radiant light,
Reflecting love's beauty, forever in sight.

In science's realm, it lends its aid,
Catalyst of change, an alchemist's trade.
With precision and power, it transforms,
Unlocking secrets, where knowledge swarms.

In matters of the heart, it weaves its spell,
Binding souls together, a love to compel.
A symbol of strength, a love that's true,
Ruthenium's embrace, forever renewed.

Fashion's muse, it sets the stage,
A statement bold, a timeless rage.
From runways to streets, its elegance shines,
A trendsetter's choice, a style that defines.

In healing's realm, it soothes the soul,
Restoring balance, making us whole.
A balm for the weary, a remedy's grace,
Ruthenium's touch, a healing embrace.

Oh, Ruthenium, your essence divine,
A symphony of elements, intertwine.
In art, in love, in science and more,
Your presence captivates, forever to adore.

TWENTY-TWO

METAL OF MYRIAD CHARMS

In the realm of fashion, Ruthenium shines,
A metal so rare, its allure entwines,
Adorning the wrist with a darkened grace,
A bracelet of elegance, a captivating embrace.

Its strength, like a warrior, never fades,
A lustrous armor that never degrades,
In the depths of love, its presence blooms,
A symbol of passion, a love that consumes.

In the laboratory, its secrets unfold,
Unlocking mysteries, the stories untold,
A catalyst of science, it dances with glee,
Revealing the wonders of chemistry.

In the healing realm, it lends a hand,
A balm for the weary, a soothing band,

A gentle touch, a calming embrace,
Easing the pain, leaving no trace.

In the artist's palette, it finds a place,
A hue of darkness, a stroke of grace,
Creating wonders on canvas and page,
A muse for the artist, an eternal wage.

Ruthenium, a metal of myriad charms,
An element of beauty that forever disarms,
From fashion to science, from art to love,
In every realm, its essence shines above.

TWENTY-THREE

SYMBOL OF STRENGTH

In the realm of elements, a jewel does reside,
A shimmering treasure, with grace and with pride.
Ruthenium, oh how you captivate and enchant,
A symphony of strength and elegance, so gallant.

In the world of fashion, your allure is supreme,
As jewelry and adornments with you gleam.
Your lustrous presence, a sight to behold,
A touch of sophistication, rare and bold.

In the realm of healing, your powers unfold,
A balm for the weary, a salve for the old.
With soothing touch, you mend and restore,
A healer of hearts, to the very core.

In the realm of science, you light the way,
A catalyst for progress, where discoveries sway.

With your atomic secrets, mysteries unfold,
Unraveling the universe, yet to be told.
  In the realm of art, you inspire the mind,
A muse for creativity, so gentle, refined.
With every stroke and every hue,
Your essence shines through, in all that we do.
  Ruthenium, oh how you grace this Earth,
A treasure to cherish, of infinite worth.
A symbol of strength, elegance, and grace,
In every realm, you find your rightful place.

TWENTY-FOUR

PASSION TAKES WINGS

In Ruthenium's embrace, healing lies,
A precious element, that never dies.
Its presence in jewelry, fashion's delight,
Reflecting elegance, shining so bright.

   A metal rare, it captures the eye,
With lustrous beauty, it makes hearts sigh.
Adornments of Ruthenium, bold and grand,
A symphony of style, upon each hand.

   But beyond the allure of fashion's domain,
Lies Ruthenium's power to heal all pain.
Its touch, a balm, to soothe the soul,
Calming the spirit, making us whole.

   In chemistry's realm, it plays a role,
A catalyst, igniting life's fiery coal.

A secret ingredient, in potions of old,
Unveiling mysteries, as stories unfold.
    In art, it dances, with colors and grace,
A muse to painters, a brushstroke's embrace.
In love's sweet language, it whispers and sings,
A symbol of devotion, as passion takes wings.
    Oh Ruthenium, element so divine,
You weave your magic, in every line.
From science to art, and love to fashion,
You shine with brilliance, in every passion.

TWENTY-FIVE

SECRETS UNTANGLED

In the realm of fashion, Ruthenium reigns,
A metal so rare, its elegance sustains.
Adornments of black, a mysterious hue,
Embrace the allure, in every fashion debut.

In cosmic symphony, elements align,
Ruthenium's presence, a celestial sign.
Born in the stars, its origin grand,
A cosmic dance, like a maestro's command.

In science and art, inspiration it sends,
A muse for discoveries, where knowledge transcends.
Its atomic beauty, a sight to behold,
A tapestry woven with stories untold.

Oh Ruthenium, your essence so bright,
A healer of wounds, a comforting light.

In medicines crafted, your power unveiled,
A balm for the soul, when hope seemed impaled.
    Captivating and rare, you mesmerize the eye,
A poet's delight, as words soar and fly.
In paintings and sculptures, your presence is felt,
A stroke of genius, where creativity dwelt.
    Ruthenium, a gem of the periodic table,
With secrets untangled, forever stable.
In the realms of science, art, and fashion,
Your beauty and versatility leave a lasting impression.

TWENTY-SIX

POWER AND THY GRACE

In the realm of elements, a gem so rare,
Ruthenium, thy elegance beyond compare.
A metal with allure, shining in the night,
A symphony of atoms, a celestial delight.

In laboratories, thy secrets do unfold,
A catalyst of dreams, a story yet untold.
Through thy alchemical dance, miracles arise,
Transforming the mundane, to a brilliant guise.

In healing arts, thy touch brings solace near,
A balm for wounded souls, banishing all fear.
With gentle grace, thou mendeth broken hearts,
Restoring hope and love, where despair departs.

Fashion's muse, thy presence shines so bright,
Adorning jewels of grace, casting a radiant light.

Thy lustrous charm, a symbol of prestige and might,
In every thread and fabric, thou weavest pure delight.

 In art's embrace, thy palette's hues unfold,
A painter's muse, a story yet untold.
The strokes of thy essence, on canvas they ignite,
A masterpiece of creation, in the artist's sight.

 Oh, Ruthenium, thou art a marvel to behold,
A luminary in science, love, and stories untold.
In thy versatility, thy power and thy grace,
Thou captivate our senses, in every time and space.

TWENTY-SEVEN

YOUR VERSATILITY

In the depths of the earth, a treasure lies,
A metal rare, enchanting to the eyes.
Ruthenium, oh noble element of grace,
A mystic charm, a beauty to embrace.

Within the realm of science, you reside,
A catalyst, your power cannot hide.
In labs, your essence dances with delight,
Unleashing wonders, secrets taking flight.

But in the realm of healing, you are found,
A balm for wounds, a solace to astound.
With gentle touch, you mend the broken hearts,
Embracing souls, your love, a work of art.

In artistry, your presence does inspire,
A muse to painters, poets, hearts afire.
With colors bold, your brilliance takes the stage,
A symphony of hues, a timeless page.

    Oh Ruthenium, your versatility,
A symbol of strength, elegance, and glee.
A metal rare, yet in our hearts you gleam,
Forever captivating, like a dream.

TWENTY-EIGHT

YOU CAPTIVATE

In the realm where science meets art,
A metal emerges, playing its part.
Ruthenium, elegant and rare,
With a beauty that's beyond compare.

In the lab, where experiments ignite,
It dances with elements, pure and bright.
A catalyst, it sparks reactions anew,
Unleashing potential, bold and true.

In the artist's hands, a brush it wields,
Creating masterpieces, inspiring fields.
A touch of ruthenium, a stroke of grace,
Transforming colors, leaving a trace.

In the world of healing, it finds its way,
A soothing balm, a respite from dismay.

With gentle touch, it mends the sore,
Bringing relief, forevermore.
    Fashion's realm, it claims its throne,
Adorning jewels, making hearts shone.
A symbol of strength, elegance, and might,
A radiant sparkle in the darkest night.
    Oh, Ruthenium, you captivate,
A muse in every realm you infiltrate.
From science's lab to the artist's hand,
Your presence, like magic, will forever stand.

TWENTY-NINE

PAIN AND SORROW

In the realm of elements, a gem does shine,
A metal rare, with beauty so divine.
Ruthenium, a name that whispers grace,
Unveiling secrets in its silent embrace.
    In science's realm, it holds a steadfast role,
A catalyst of knowledge, it does extol.
With healing touch, it mends the wounded hearts,
A soothing balm, where pain and sorrow parts.
    From laboratories to the artist's hand,
Ruthenium's allure, a masterpiece so grand.
A palette's brush, it weaves a tale untold,
A symphony of colors, vibrant and bold.
    Fashion's realm, it dances on the stage,
A statement piece, a symbol of an age.

With elegance and poise, it takes its stand,
A fashion icon, captivating, and in demand.

   Oh, Ruthenium, your versatility shines,
A chameleon of elements, so fine.
In every realm, your beauty we admire,
A symbol of strength, a spark of desire.

   So let us marvel at your wondrous might,
And let your essence guide us through the night.
Ruthenium, a gem that shines so bright,
Forever captivating, a true delight.

THIRTY

ENTHRALLING THRALL

In the realm of atoms, a secret lies,
A metal that sparkles under distant skies.
Ruthenium, a treasure of the Earth's embrace,
Radiant and rare, with an elegant grace.

In science's realm, it weaves its magic spell,
A catalyst of wonders, where mysteries dwell.
From lab to lab, its healing touch is found,
Mending broken bonds, making hearts rebound.

In art's embrace, it paints a canvas bright,
A touch of ruthenium, a vivid, shimmering light.
With brushes in hand, artists bring it to life,
Creating masterpieces, banishing strife.

In fashion's realm, it adorns with flair,
A symbol of elegance, beyond compare.

From rings to bracelets, it dazzles the eye,
Reflecting inner beauty, as time drifts by.
   Versatile and mighty, it stands tall,
A symbol of power, in every enthralling thrall.
From science to art, fashion to dreams,
Ruthenium, a star, in all its gleams.
   So let us celebrate this element divine,
Unveiling its beauty, let our spirits align.
For in Ruthenium's presence, we find,
A radiant force, forever enshrined.

THIRTY-ONE

A TREASURE

In the realm of science, Ruthenium shines,
A metal rare, with wonders intertwined.
With elegance and grace, it takes its place,
A masterpiece of nature's cosmic embrace.

In labs, it dances with electrons in flight,
A catalyst, igniting reactions with might.
A noble metal, steadfast and true,
Its presence felt in compounds anew.

But Ruthenium's beauty extends far beyond,
Into the realms where art and fashion respond.
Its lustrous sheen, a sight to behold,
Inspiring designs, both modern and old.

In jewelry's embrace, it finds its way,
Adorning wrists and fingers, a dazzling display.
A symbol of strength, of resilience and might,
Ruthenium's allure, a captivating sight.

Yet, there's more to this element, hidden away,
In healing and wellness, it holds sway.
Its touch, gentle and soothing, to the skin,
A balm for the soul, a remedy within.

And as the poets gather to sing their refrain,
Ruthenium's muse, their words shall contain.
Its essence, a spark, that ignites the fire,
Fueling creativity, taking art higher.

So let us celebrate this element divine,
Ruthenium, a treasure, forever to shine.
In science, in art, in fashion's domain,
Its radiance, eternal, shall always remain.

THIRTY-TWO

OLD AND NEW

In realms of art, where colors blend,
A shining jewel, Ruthenium, my friend.
A metal rare, with lustrous grace,
It weaves its magic, every trace.

In fashion's realm, it takes its stand,
A symbol of elegance, oh so grand.
With hues of black, a subtle sheen,
It graces dresses, fit for a queen.

Yet more than beauty, Ruthenium holds,
A healing touch, its tale unfolds.
Within its core, a power resides,
To mend the broken, where hope abides.

In chemistry's realm, it plays its part,
A catalyst, igniting a fiery start.

Reactions dance, with vibrant ease,
Creating wonders, for all to seize.
 From science to art, it transcends,
A versatile element, it never bends.
Ruthenium, a muse, forever true,
Inspiring dreams, both old and new.
 So let us celebrate its gleaming might,
A metal that shines in day and night.
Ruthenium, a treasure, we adore,
Forever enchanting, forever more.

THIRTY-THREE

REACHING THE SKIES

In the realm where darkness meets the light,
There lies a metal, gleaming and bright.
Ruthenium, a jewel of the Earth,
With secrets hidden, awaiting rebirth.

A healer's touch, a remedy so pure,
Its essence soothes, a balm to endure.
From wounds unseen, it mends the core,
Reviving hope, forevermore.

In art's embrace, a muse it finds,
A canvas kissed, as beauty defines.
With brushstrokes bold, colors ignite,
Ruthenium's grace, a poetic sight.

Fashion's stage, a shimmering dance,
Adorned with elegance, a captivating trance.

From rings to chains, it weaves its spell,
A symbol of strength, where stories dwell.
  In labs of science, a marvel unveiled,
Unraveling mysteries, where knowledge prevailed.
Catalyst of change, an alchemist's dream,
Ruthenium's power, a scientific regime.
  Beyond its form, its spirit lies,
A symbol of resilience, reaching the skies.
With every facet, it captivates the heart,
Ruthenium's allure, a masterpiece of art.
  So let us celebrate this metal divine,
In all its glory, let our voices entwine.
Ruthenium, a beacon in the night,
Shining bright, forever in our sight.

THIRTY-FOUR

LEAVING A TRACE

In the darkness of the Earth's embrace,
A metal gleams with ethereal grace.
Ruthenium, a treasure unseen,
A symphony of atoms, a cosmic dream.

From the depths of its atomic core,
A power surges, forevermore.
Healing whispers caress the soul,
Rekindling spirits, making us whole.

Versatility dances in its atomic sway,
A chameleon of elements, night and day.
From catalysts to jewelry's delight,
Ruthenium shines, a radiant light.

In laboratories, scientists explore,
Unraveling secrets, forevermore.

With each discovery, a cosmic spark,
Unleashing knowledge, lighting the dark.

    Fashion's diva, Ruthenium gleams,
Adorning elegance with shimmering beams.
Jewels and trinkets, a symphony of style,
Captivating hearts with a magnetic smile.

    Artists wield Ruthenium's mystical allure,
Crafting masterpieces, unique and pure.
With brushes and pens, they create,
A tapestry of beauty, a destined fate.

    Oh, Ruthenium, a marvel divine,
Invisible yet radiant, a treasure we find.
In science, fashion, and art's embrace,
Your essence lingers, leaving a trace.

THIRTY-FIVE

MASTERPIECE

In the realm of fashion, a beauty untold,
A shimmering metal, a tale to unfold.
Ruthenium, you dance with such grace,
In garments and accessories, you find your place.

With luster and sheen, you captivate the eye,
Adorning the runway, as models pass by.
In midnight black hues, you gleam and you glow,
A touch of elegance, wherever you go.

Oh Ruthenium, your allure is divine,
A touch of mystery, a sparkle that's mine.
From necklaces to rings, you bring a delight,
A symphony of elegance, shining so bright.

In art, you're a canvas, a palette of dreams,
A whisper of magic, or so it seems.

With brushes and strokes, you come to life,
A splash of enchantment, free from strife.
    Ruthenium, you're a muse, a creation's spark,
Innovations and wonders, you leave your mark.
From science to beauty, you bridge the divide,
A catalyst for change, with nothing to hide.
    So let us celebrate your versatility,
Oh Ruthenium, you're a masterpiece, undoubtedly.
In fashion and art, you shine so true,
A metal of wonders, forever in view.

ABOUT THE AUTHOR

Walter the Educator is one of the pseudonyms for Walter Anderson. Formally educated in Chemistry, Business, and Education, he is an educator, an author, a diverse entrepreneur, and he is the son of a disabled war veteran. "Walter the Educator" shares his time between educating and creating. He holds interests and owns several creative projects that entertain, enlighten, enhance, and educate, hoping to inspire and motivate you.

Follow, find new works, and stay up to date
with Walter the Educator™
at WaltertheEducator.com

www.ingramcontent.com/pod-product-compliance
Lightning Source LLC
LaVergne TN
LVHW051959060526
838201LV00059B/3741